The **TINY TAXMAN**

Wouldn't it be lovely to have lots of money?

Zacc had a job that made him very rich. All he had to do was sit at a table, and people came up to him and gave him money.

Great eh?

Some of the coins had to be given to the surly soldiers protecting him, and the rest went into his pockets.

Zacchaeus (that was his full name) worked for the Romans as a taxman.

The Roman army had conquered his land some years before.

His neighbours hated him. Traitors working for the enemy are always despised.

Every time Zacc saw money or heard the clinking of coins, his eyes flashed like the lights on a fruit machine. His jaw dropped open. He'd hit the jackpot again!

The funny thing was, the more money he got... the more parties he held... the more miserable he became.

Even his promotion to chief taxman didn't really satisfy him, deep down. There was an ache inside that just wouldn't go away.

One day he overheard someone talking about a Man who worked miracles and spoke about true happiness. This amazing Man was passing through Jericho that very day. A huge crowd surrounded Jesus and his disciples as he moved through the streets of Jericho, for what turned out to be the last time.

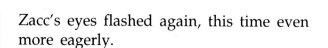

Zacc's eyes flashed again, this time even more eagerly.

This was his big chance and he wasn't going to miss it.

Because he was only a small man, he tried to push his way to the front of the crowd. But when the people saw it was Zacchaeus, they bunched up together to keep him out. As he looked up into their angry faces, Zacc changed his mind, quickly!

Suddenly, he remembered the sycamore trees that lined the road. Running as fast as his little legs would carry him, he shinned up the nearest tree and pulled the leaves around him.

He could just hear Jesus telling the people that God wanted them to live good, honest lives, putting God first. The longer he listened to God's Son, the Lord Jesus, the more guilty Zacc felt.

Then, as the crowd passed under Zacc's hiding place, the worst possible thing happened! Jesus stopped and looked straight up at Zacchaeus. The crowd too followed his eyes.

Poor Zacc saw a sea of eyes staring up at him.

Was Jesus going to let the crowd punish him? Was he about to be killed?

As Zacc gazed into the eyes of the Saviour, he realised that Jesus knew all about his wickedness and yet still loved him.

Zacc nearly fell out of his tree when he heard the Lord ask him to come down quickly because he wanted to stay at his house.

Without sparing a second, Zacc slipped down the tree faster than a fireman sliding down his pole.

Jesus smiled at the tiny taxman. He knew that Zacchaeus had made up his mind to live God's way.

The crowd grumbled about such a good man going to a traitor's house. But Zacc took the Lord to his home and soon found out that love, holiness and forgiveness were the greatest joys of his life.

To show that he really meant to change his ways, he told the Lord that he was going to give half of his money to the poor, immediately.

The news was all over town the next day! Beggars, orphans, widows and the sick all received money from Zacc. Much more than that, Zacc promised to pay back those he had cheated with the money he had left.

Zacc had told the Lord that he would repay everyone he had cheated four times over! So someone who had lost four coins received how many back?

That's right, sixteen.

Can you imagine what Mrs. Isaacs might have said when Zacc came to the door? "Clear off! You're trying to trick us again."

"No, I'm a changed man," he would have answered, "Jesus is my Master now, not money."

Poor Mrs Abrahams may well have passed out with shock! Everybody in town was amazed at the change in his life. Zacchaeus had found a real reason for living. He saw how foolish he had been in the past. Now he had found a treasure far greater than all the money that had passed through his hands.

Have you realised that there are more important things in this world than having "loadsamoney"? Jesus told his disciples that having all the wealth in the world is no good to you if you lose out on eternal life.

The Lord Jesus wants you to trust him. Has there been a time when you prayed to Jesus to ask him to forgive you for the wrong things you have done? Are you sure that you are a real Christian? If not, maybe you should sit down somewhere quiet for a few minutes and think very carefully about God.

GOD LOVED SINNERS ENOUGH TO SEND HIS SON JESUS TO DIE FOR THEM.

JESUS DIED IN THE PLACE OF THOSE WHO TRUST IN HIM.

GOD PUNISHED JESUS INSTEAD OF THEM AND TOOK AWAY THEIR SINS.

GOD NOW ASKS YOU IF YOU ARE REALLY SORRY ENOUGH TO TURN AWAY FROM SIN.

If you REALLY are sorry, read the following prayer to see if you could say that to God.

Dear God,

I am really sorry for my sin. Thank you for your amazing love for me.

I believe that you sent Jesus to die for sinners. Please forgive my sins, for Jesus' sake. I give you my life, because you gave your life for me. Help me to live for you throughout all my life. I want to be saved and become your child. I ask all this in Jesus' name. Amen.

Jesus' words were true in the case of Zacchaeus, "Today salvation has come to this house."

If you are willing to ask the Lord to forgive you, you will be saved too.

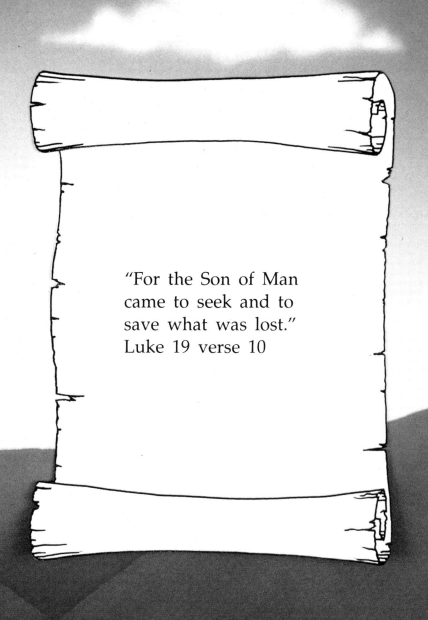

"For the Son of Man came to seek and to save what was lost." Luke 19 verse 10

The TINY TAXMAN
The Story of ZACCHAEUS

Here is the complete story from Luke chapter 19.

Jesus entered Jericho and was passing through. A man was there by the name of Zacchaeus; he was a chief tax collector and was wealthy. He wanted to see who Jesus was, but being a short man he could not, because of the crowd. So he ran ahead and climbed a sycamore-fig tree to see him, since Jesus was coming that way.

When Jesus reached the spot, he looked up and said to him, "Zacchaeus, come down immediately. I must stay at your house today." So he came down at once and welcomed him gladly.

All the people saw this and began to mutter, "He has gone to be the guest of a 'sinner'."

But Zacchaeus stood up and said to the Lord, "Look, Lord! Here and now I give half of my possessions to the poor, and if I have cheated anybody out of anything, I will pay back four times the amount."